£ 4,99

D1150926

*Flash* *vise*

124055

AS Business Studies

Philip Allan Updates, an imprint of Hodder Education, an Hachette UK company, Market Place, Deddington, Oxfordshire OX15 0SE

Orders

Bookpoint Ltd, 130 Milton Park, Abingdon, Oxfordshire OX14 4SB
tel: 01235 827720   fax: 01235 400454   e-mail: uk.orders@bookpoint.co.uk

Lines are open 9.00 a.m.–5.00 p.m., Monday to Saturday, with a 24-hour message answering service. You can also order through our website: www.philipallan.co.uk

© Philip Allan Updates 2010
ISBN 978-1-4441-1542-0

Impression number 5 4 3 2 1
Year   2014   2013   2012   2011   2010

Printed in Spain

Hachette UK's policy is to use papers that are natural, renewable and recyclable products and made from wood grown in sustainable forests. The logging and manufacturing processes are expected to conform to the environmental regulations of the country of origin.

P01753

Unit 1

1 Resources
2 Opportunity cost
3 Risk
4 Reward
5 Transformation process
6 Adding value
7 Primary sector
8 Start-up objectives
9 Entrepreneur
10 What is a business start up?
11 Start-up location
12 Business failure
13 Business Link
14 Franchisee
15 Franchisor
16 Patent
17 Copyright
18 Trademark
19 Business plan
20 Demand
21 A market
22 Market niche
23 Market size
24 Market share
25 Market segment
26 Market growth
27 Negative market growth
28 Market research
29 Sample
30 Random sample
31 Secondary market research
32 Sole trader
33 Partnership
34 Private limited company
35 Limited liability
36 Sources of finance
37 Internal sources of finance
38 Ordinary shares
39 Venture capital
40 Employee
41 Temporary employees
42 Management consultants
43 Variable and fixed costs
44 Total costs
45 Total revenue
46 Profit
47 Break-even output
48 Contribution per unit
49 Total contribution
50 Margin of safety

Unit 2

Resources

Q1 Which of the following is not a resource: land, labour, profits, capital equipment?

Q2 Which of the following is not an output: goods, labour, services, waste products?

Q3 The aim of business is to produce inputs worth more than outputs. True or false?

Q4 Resources are limited at any time. True or false?

ANSWERS

resources are inputs used up in
the production process

A1 profits; this is an objective

A2 labour; this is an input

A3 false; the aim is to produce outputs worth more than the inputs

A4 true

***examiner's* note** If resources are managed effectively, a business can
produce more outputs with fewer inputs. This increases efficiency and can
make the business more competitive.

 ANSWERS

Opportunity cost

Q1 If a firm invests in a new production process, which of the following is the opportunity cost: (a) the cost of new equipment; (b) the expected revenues; (c) the interest that may have been earned if the money had been left in the bank?

Q2 What might be the opportunity cost of going to university?

Q3 Why is there an opportunity cost involved in holding stock?

Q4 What would increase the opportunity cost of holding cash?

ANSWERS

the benefits given up by undertaking an activity

A1 (c)

A2 the money that could be earned by getting a job straight from school (however, the future earnings as a graduate may outweigh these losses)

A3 the money invested in stock could be used elsewhere, e.g. saved in a bank and earning interest

A4 the cash could be invested, e.g. in a bank, and the cost of holding cash would increase with higher interest rates

***examiner's* note** All decisions involve an opportunity cost. Whenever you are considering an action, it is worth thinking about what else you could be doing with the resources.

Whether a decision made by a manager is the 'right' one depends in part on the opportunity cost — what else could have been done instead? Earning £20m may be impressive, but not if you could have earned £40m elsewhere.

 ANSWERS

Risk

Q1 What are the risks of setting up in business?

Q2 State two possible rewards of setting up in business.

Q3 Why do entrepreneurs take risks?

Q4 How can entrepreneurs reduce the risks of setting up?

ANSWERS

the chance or probability of something going wrong

A1 the business may fail; this may affect your pride, your reputation and your ability to raise finance and find partners in the future

A2 profits; personal satisfaction

A3 to gain rewards; to see if they can achieve something

A4 by seeking professional advice first; by researching the market thoroughly

***examiner's* note** All business decisions involve a risk; the important questions are how high these risks are and what the rewards are in return.

(3) **ANSWERS**

Reward

Q1 Entrepreneurs are risk takers. True or false?

Q2 Entrepreneurs must set up as a private limited company. True or false?

Q3 Many start ups do not earn a profit in the first year. True or false?

Q4 Entrepreneurs can automatically protect their ideas. True or false?

ANSWERS

the positive return gained from an action

A1 true

A2 false

A3 true

A4 false

***examiner's* note** Simply earning a reward is not enough. Entrepreneurs will need to make enough profit to make the venture worthwhile. Making £5,000 a year, for example, may not be enough if you work 40 hours a week for 50 weeks a year.

 ANSWERS

Transformation process

Q1 What is meant by primary production?

Q2 What is meant by secondary production?

Q3 What is meant by tertiary production?

Q4 What is the aim of the transformation process?

ANSWERS

the process of converting inputs into outputs

A1 the first stage of the production process, e.g. extractive industries and farming

A2 this refers to businesses involved in manufacturing or construction, e.g. car producers

A3 this refers to business involved in services, e.g. schools and management consultants

A4 to generate outputs worth more than the cost of inputs used up in the process

***examiner's* note** Managing the transformation process effectively can mean that resources are used efficiently and that the products provided are of a high quality.

Adding value

Q1 Construction is part of the primary sector. True or false?

Q2 Education is part of the primary sector. True or false?

Q3 Most businesses in the UK are in the tertiary sector. True or false?

Q4 Farming is part of the primary sector. True or false?

ANSWERS

the process by which outputs are produced
that are worth more than the inputs used up

A1 false

A2 false

A3 true

A4 true

***examiner's* note** All businesses aim to add value, and entrepreneurs are
constantly looking for new markets and new needs that they can satisfy.

Primary sector

Q1 Which of the following activities is not in the primary sector: (a) oil refining; (b) fishing; (c) publishing? What sector is it in?

Q2 Explain what is meant by the secondary and tertiary sectors.

Q3 Which of the following is an example of a primary sector business: (a) a chocolate manufacturer; (b) a farm; (c) a school?

Q4 In terms of employment and income, is the primary sector relatively large or relatively small in the UK?

ANSWERS

A1 (c); tertiary

A2 secondary sector: firms in the economy that convert raw materials into finished goods; tertiary sector: businesses supplying services

A3 (b)

A4 relatively small

***examiner's* note** The primary sector often produces 'commodities', e.g. food crops. It can be hard to differentiate these products, so profit margins can be low. In contrast, in the market for cola drinks, for example, a lot of money is spent differentiating brands (e.g. Pepsi vs Coca-Cola) to make demand less price sensitive.

Some argue that the government should support primary firms more because it protects a way of life and keeps production of essential products going, but this would have an opportunity cost and may encourage inefficiency.

 7 ANSWERS

Start-up objectives

Q1 State two typical objectives for a start-up business.

Q2 State two advantages of setting objectives.

Q3 Most start ups survive and grow into big businesses. True or false?

Q4 Entrepreneurs help provide new products for a market. True or false?

ANSWERS ▶▶

the targets that entrepreneurs set when starting a new venture

A1 survival; ensuring there is sufficient cash flow; break-even

A2 helps coordinate resources; helps measure progress against these targets; helps people understand the priorities and make better decisions

A3 false

A4 true

***examiner's* note** An objective can provide a target which helps managers plan and organise resources. However, managers still have to take appropriate actions to meet these targets.

Entrepreneur

Q1 State two reasons why someone might start their own business.

Q2 State two possible problems of starting your own business.

Q3 State two sources of ideas for your new business.

Q4 Name one entrepreneur and their business.

ANSWERS

someone who is willing to take a risk to start their own business or project

A1 to keep the rewards for themselves; to make their own decisions; to be their own boss; to make sure they have a job

A2 lack of finance; lack of experience in some areas; power of established firms

A3 own idea; own experiences; copying an existing idea

A4 Branson and Virgin; Dunstone and Carphone Warehouse; Levi Roots and his Reggae Reggae Sauce

***examiner's* note** The motives and objectives vary from entrepreneur to entrepreneur. You need to understand these to be able to judge if it is a success or not.

 ANSWERS

What is a business start up?

Q1 All businesses start as sole traders. True or false?

Q2 All business start ups are financed by the entrepreneur. True or false?

Q3 All businesses are companies. True or false?

Q4 Most start ups are financed by the government. True or false?

ANSWERS

a new business being created

A1 false

A2 false

A3 false

A4 false

examiner's **note** Finding the finance to start a business can be difficult. Banks are often reluctant to lend because of the risks of failure and entrepreneurs may not have many of their own resources.

Start-up location

Q1 State two factors influencing a start-up location.

Q2 State two reasons why a start-up location matters.

Q3 State two difficulties finding the best start-up location.

Q4 State two types of business that need to be near their customers.

ANSWERS

A1 costs; personal preferences; type of business; where competitors are located

A2 affects likely demand and costs (and therefore break-even)

A3 costs; lack of experience; best locations have already gone

A4 coffee shop; fast-food shop; clothes shops

***examiner's* note** The location of a start up depends very much on the type of business; many online businesses have been started from people's bedrooms!

Business failure

Q1 State two reasons why new businesses often fail.

Q2 State two possible ways a new business idea might be protected.

Q3 State three qualities an entrepreneur may need to succeed.

ANSWERS

A1 lack of finance; lack of skills; lack of experience; lack of power in the market; lack of customer awareness; wrong location

A2 depends on the idea, but it may be protected with a patent or trademark

A3 perseverance; commitment; understanding of different areas of business; ability to negotiate; a vision of where the business is going; flexibility; planning skills

examiner's **note** Many new businesses fail due to a lack of experience or a lack of market power. The first few years of a business are often its most difficult.

Business Link

Q1 Why might a government encourage entrepreneurs?

Q2 How might the government encourage entrepreneurs?

Q3 State two ways the government can affect business success.

Q4 All new businesses need a licence. True or false?

ANSWERS ▶▶

A1 because entrepreneurs provide jobs, new products and competition; they reduce unemployment and they pay tax

A2 by providing advice and contacts with experts; by guaranteeing loans

A3 by affecting the economy; through laws; through its own purchasing

A4 false

***examiner's* note** Governments generally support start ups because of the jobs they create and products they offer; however, this involves a commitment of resources and therefore an opportunity cost.

Franchisee

Q1 State two possible problems in buying a franchise.

Q2 State two factors you might consider when choosing whether to buy a franchise.

Q3 All franchisees are private limited companies. True or false?

Q4 Franchises are mainly owned by the government. True or false?

ANSWERS

a franchisee buys a franchise from a franchisor

A1 the cost of buying it and the percentage of revenue paid to the franchisor; franchisees may resent the control of the franchisor and would prefer to pursue their own policies

A2 the reputation and track record of the franchise; the costs of the purchase; the alternatives; the support and advice offered by the franchisor

A3 false

A4 false

examiner's note Remember, not all franchises are successful; you need to check carefully the track record of the franchise and try to be sure that the other franchises will not damage the brand in the future.

(14) **ANSWERS**

Franchisor

Q1 State two reasons for buying a franchise.

Q2 What costs are involved in buying a franchise?

Q3 What is a franchisee?

Q4 What support might you get from a franchisor?

ANSWERS

a business that sells the right to use its name and products to another business

A1 provides an established business idea; brings the support of the franchisor and other franchisees, which may reduce the risk of failure

A2 there is usually an initial fee to buy it and a percentage of turnover is paid to the franchisor

A3 the franchisee buys the business name and product from a franchisor

A4 may get advice and training; may share marketing costs and get the actual product and brand

examiner's note A franchise can be appealing because it reduces risk but it also means there is less freedom than when running your own business; you must consider if you are happy to lose some of your profits and independence before buying a franchise.

 **ANSWERS**

Patent

Q1 Does a patent have to be registered? Why does this matter?

Q2 A patent lasts for ever. True or false?

Q3 How can the patent system benefit a business?

Q4 To gain a patent, an idea must be which of the following:
(a) freely available to everyone; (b) truly new; (c) related to
existing products?

ANSWERS

legal protection for a new product or production process

A1 yes; it means that other firms can keep up to date with developments, and also a cost is involved in registering the patent

A2 false; it usually lasts for 15 years

A3 can license its own patent; protects its inventions from imitators; can learn about other firms' developments through their patents

A4 (b)

***examiner's* note** The success of a new product may be helped by taking out a patent (if this is possible) to protect it from competition. However, it still has to be marketed effectively and meet a need if it is to be successful. Registering a patent in the UK is not especially expensive, but the inventor then has to register in other countries and be prepared to take legal action if the patent is ignored. This can be costly and time consuming.

Copyright

Q1 Does a copyright have to be registered with the government?

Q2 Which of the following would be copyrightable: (a) a new production process; (b) a new product; (c) a new song? Explain.

Q3 How does the copyright system benefit writers and musicians?

Q4 An individual is only allowed one copyright. True or false?

ANSWERS

legal protection for authors, composers and artists against copying of their work

A1 no — these rights are held automatically

A2 (c); the others would have to be patented

A3 their music, plays, books or films cannot simply be copied without a fee, which encourages more creativity

A4 false

***examiner's* note** A copyright can help people gain rewards for their work, but this does not mean that the work will sell. The level of sales will depend on a range of factors, such as the quality and the effectiveness of the marketing. Copyrights act as an incentive for creativity and innovation because people know their work will have some protection. Patents have the same impact with regard to new products and processes.

Trademark

Q1 A trademark has to be registered. True or false?

Q2 A trademark protects music and literature? True or false?

Q3 To defend your trademark, you take another business to court. True or false?

Q4 Identify three distinctive trademarks you know.

ANSWERS

provides legal protection for a design or
logo that identifies a product or business

A1 true

A2 false; this is a copyright

A3 true

A4 Apple, McDonald's, Coca-Cola or any other you know

examiner's note Even if you protect your idea or logo, others can copy it
and you then have to sue them, which can take time and be expensive.

Business plan

Q1 State two groups that might want to look at a firm's business plan. Explain why each group might be interested.

Q2 A plan may estimate future cash inflows and outflows. This is called a c............-f............ f..................... State one benefit of having this.

Q3 A business plan may include the break-even output. How could the break-even output be reduced?

Q4 What else might be contained in a business plan apart from break-even?

ANSWERS))

a report detailing an organisation's expected activities, incomes and expenditures

A1 potential investors/bank — to decide whether or not it is likely to be a good investment; employees — to see where the business is heading

A2 cash-flow forecast; can prepare for times of low cash flow, e.g. arrange an overdraft

A3 by cutting costs or increasing the sales price

A4 marketing plan (including sales forecast); cash-flow forecast; projected profit and loss; details of required finance; information on the entrepreneurs

***examiner's* note** A business plan does not guarantee success, but it may help managers to think ahead and anticipate possible problems; it may also help the firm raise finance. The success of a business plan depends on how accurate it is, what is in it, whether it is implemented effectively and whether it is updated.

(19) ANSWERS

Demand

Q1 Which function of a business aims to identify customer needs?

Q2 If something is wanted, it is always worth providing. True or false?

Q3 State three factors that are likely to influence demand for something.

Q4 Why might the demand for business studies textbooks fall?

ANSWERS

the amount of a product that customers are willing and able to buy

A1 marketing

A2 false; it depends on costs and the price people are prepared to pay — it may not be profitable

A3 income; prices; number of buyers; the prices of alternatives; competitors' actions; the season

A4 fewer students studying the subject; more online resources or other forms of learning resources

***examiner's* note** Businesses will usually try to increase demand but sometimes they may try to make it more stable (e.g. less seasonal) or even reduce demand if they want to avoid queues or waiting lists.

A market

Q1 State two products for which there is a seasonal demand.

Q2 Is demand for salt likely to be sensitive to income?

Q3 Is demand to join a health and leisure club likely to be sensitive to income?

Q4 How can a business influence demand for its products?

ANSWERS

A1 ice cream; fireworks; sunglasses; Christmas cards

A2 no

A3 yes

A4 through its marketing activities, e.g. promotion, pricing, distribution and changing the product itself

***examiner's* note** The factors influencing demand vary from product to product; demand for clothes may be influenced by fashion, demand for ice cream by the weather and demand for cars by income.

Market niche

Q1 State two factors an entrepreneur might consider when assessing a business idea.

Q2 State two difficulties of being an entrepreneur.

Q3 Why is knowing there is demand for a product not enough to be sure it will be a profitable business idea?

ANSWERS

a small segment of the market

A1 whether it matches the entrepreneur's interests and strengths; whether the market is big enough and potentially profitable; how easy it is to protect the idea

A2 can be stressful; can require many different skills; there is a high risk of failure

A3 depends on costs; demand can change; there may be too much competition

***examiner's* note** A market niche creates some risks because there are likely to be relatively few customers; if you lose a customer, this could have a major effect on demand.

Market size

Q1 A market has increased in size from £2m to £2.4m. What is the percentage market growth?

Q2 A market that was worth £200,000 has increased in size by 30%. What is it now worth?

Q3 State four reasons why a market might increase in size.

Q4 The sales of one product as a percentage of the total market sales is known as its m.............. s..............

ANSWERS

A1 $\dfrac{2.4 - 2}{2} \times 100 = 20\%$

A2 $\dfrac{30}{100} \times £200{,}000 = £60{,}000$

value is now £200,000 + £60,000 = £260,000

A3 • greater population size   • effective marketing
   • fits with social trend   • new products creating demand

A4 market share

***examiner's* note** Sometimes markets can grow in terms of volume (i.e. the number of sales) but not in value if the price is falling.

A 'big' market may not necessarily be more attractive than a 'small' one. It depends on the competition and the firm's ability to compete in this market.

(23) ANSWERS

Market share

Q1 Sales of a particular brand are £2,000; the market sales are £20,000. What is the market share?

Q2 Brand X has 20% of a market worth £600m. What is the value of its sales?

Q3 State two possible benefits of a large market share.

Q4 State four ways in which a firm might increase its market share.

ANSWERS

sales of a product or brand relative to total market sales

A1 $\dfrac{2,000}{20,000} \times 100 = 10\%$

A2 $\dfrac{20}{100} \times £600m = £120m$

A3 • power over suppliers and distributors
   • greater brand awareness, so easier to introduce new products

A4 • lower price   • offer a USP
   • increase its promotion   • widen distribution

examiner's note More sales may not necessarily mean a bigger market share if the market as a whole is growing even faster. Increasing market share is more likely if a firm has a competitive advantage, e.g. if it can sell at a lower price or it has a unique selling proposition.

Market segment

Q1 State two ways in which a market may be segmented.

Q2 State two factors that might make a segment attractive to a firm.

Q3 State two benefits of effective segmentation.

Q4 State two reasons why a firm may not target a particular segment.

ANSWERS

a section of the market with similar needs and wants

A1 by age; by socioeconomic group; by geographical area; by gender

A2 high expected returns; limited competition; fits with firm's strengths; can protect the idea

A3 more focused marketing; less waste of resources

A4 lacks the necessary skills/resources; too much competition; low expected profits

***examiner's* note** With increasing competition, firms are always looking for new segments to target, e.g. cereals have been positioned as food to eat at night as well as in the morning. A segment is likely to be more appealing if a firm has the skills needed to succeed, if the expected returns are high and if competition is limited.

Market growth

Q1 How might a firm react to growth in demand in its market?

Q2 If a market was worth £300m and is now worth £360m, by what percentage has it grown?

Q3 State two reasons why a market may grow.

Q4 If a firm has a falling market share, can its sales increase?

ANSWERS

A1 may expand to meet the demand, put up its price if demand is high, or launch new products

A2 $\dfrac{360 - 300}{300} \times 100 = 20\%$

A3 consumers' incomes increase; better marketing; more consumers (e.g. start selling in new markets)

A4 yes, if the market is growing quickly enough

***examiner's* note** At any single moment, some markets will be growing (e.g. organic food), while others will be shrinking (e.g. high-fat products). The impact of market growth depends on whether the firm's particular segment is growing, whether it has the capacity to expand and whether growth attracts more firms to enter that market, leading to more competition.

Negative market growth

Q1 If a market has a value of £500,000 and each item sells on average for £2.50, how many units are sold?

Q2 If a market was worth £500,000 and then grows by 2%, what is it now worth?

Q3 If a market was worth £500,000 and then grows to a value of £600,000, by how much has it grown?

Q4 If a market was worth £500,000 last year and is worth £450,000 this year, what is the growth rate of the market?

ANSWERS

A1 $\dfrac{£500,000}{£2.50} = 20,000$ units

A2 $\dfrac{2}{100} \times £500,000 = £10,000$

value is now $£500,000 + £10,000 = £510,000$

A3 $\dfrac{600,000 - 500,000}{500,000} \times 100 = 20\%$

A4 $\dfrac{450,000 - 500,000}{500,000} \times 100 = \dfrac{-50,000}{500,000} \times 100 = -10\%$

***examiner's* note** The size of a market can be measured in terms of the number of units sold or the value of the sales.

Market research

Q1 How might market research help a business start up?

Q2 State two ways in which an entrepreneur may undertake market research.

Q3 When starting up, entrepreneurs are often short of money and use small sample research. Why might this be a problem?

Q4 Some entrepreneurs research their ideas by asking their friends. What are the dangers of this?

ANSWERS

the process of gathering, analysing, interpreting and presenting data relevant to marketing

A1 might help to determine the marketing mix, which segment to target and the product positioning

A2 • a survey (primary research)
   • using newspapers/journals (secondary research)

A3 the findings are less reliable

A4 they may only tell the entrepreneur what he or she wants to hear; biased results; likely to be a small sample

examiner's note Market research cannot guarantee success, but it can provide information to reduce the risk of failure. The value of market research depends on how it is conducted (e.g. the sample size) and whether it is primary or secondary (e.g. how up to date it is).

Sample

Q1 'The population' in marketing refers to everyone in the country. True or false?

Q2 State two possible reasons why samples are used in research.

Q3 A larger sample is more likely to produce accurate results than a smaller one. True or false?

Q4 Asking people questions on the street gives a random sample. True or false?

ANSWERS ▶▶

a small number of people chosen to represent the population as a whole

A1 false; it refers to everyone in the target group

A2 to save time and money

A3 true

A4 false; only those who happen to be there can be asked so each member of the population does not have an equal chance of selection

***examiner's* note** Market research can help managers to make better decisions but its reliability depends on how the data are collected and interpreted; for example, you need to consider the size and method of sampling used.

Random sample

Q1 Is a random sample likely to be used in primary or secondary research? Explain.

Q2 A non-random sample in which the interviewer finds people who meet the required characteristics is called a q...............

Q3 How can a firm increase the reliability of its findings from a sample? Explain.

Q4 Explain two uses of market research.

ANSWERS ▶▶

a sample in which every member of the population has an equal chance of selection

A1 primary; it is gathering new data

A2 quota

A3 by increasing the size of the sample so it is more representative of the population; by making sure interviewers do not use leading questions

A4 • better understanding of competition, so a better strategy can be developed
   • better understanding of customers, so the product and promotion can be improved

***examiner's* note** Remember that sampling provides information but also brings risks — the findings may not represent the population as a whole. The reliability of a sample depends on its size and how it was selected.

Secondary market research

Q1 Would surveys be used in secondary research? Explain.

Q2 Should secondary or primary research be used to help a firm find out how people may react to a new name for an existing product? Explain.

Q3 State two advantages of secondary research compared to primary.

Q4 State two sources of secondary data.

ANSWERS ▶▶

A1 no; surveys would be used to gather data for the first time, i.e. in primary research

A2 primary; the data will not have been collected before

A3 often cheaper and quicker to do

A4
- the firm's own records
- newspapers
- government statistics
- company accounts

examiner's note Secondary research is not always useful: the findings can be out of date or not in the format required by the firm. Secondary research is more likely to be used if appropriate data already exist or the firm is trying to save money.

(31) ANSWERS

Sole trader

Q1 Does a sole trader have limited or unlimited liability? Why does this matter?

Q2 Can a sole trader sell shares? Why does this matter?

Q3 State one advantage of being a sole trader rather than a company.

Q4 State one possible disadvantage of being a sole trader apart from finance and liability.

ANSWERS ▶▶

a type of organisation where the owner manages the business

A1 unlimited liability; this is risky because if anything goes wrong, sole traders can lose their personal possessions

A2 no; this restricts the ability of the business to raise funds, e.g. for expansion

A3 sole traders are their own boss and do not have to answer to shareholders, which may speed up decisions

A4 have to make all the decisions themselves — can be stressful; may lack all the required skills

***examiner's* note** An entrepreneur may prefer to remain a sole trader rather than establish a company because of greater privacy and lower administration costs. However, sole trading can be a lot of hard work and stressful.

Partnership

Q1 All partners have limited liability. True or false?

Q2 If there is no legal agreement, partners divide profits equally. True or false?

Q3 A partnership is ended when a partner leaves. True or false?

Q4 State two benefits of a partnership compared to sole trader status.

ANSWERS

when two or more people join together in a business enterprise

A1 false

A2 true

A3 true

A4 more investment; share decision making; share skills and expertise

***examiner's* note** A partnership is risky because you are liable for the actions of the other partners; if they make a mistake, you are responsible for this as well.

Private limited company

Q1 All private limited companies are family companies.
True or false? Why?

Q2 State two reasons why investors might buy shares in a company.

Q3 State two possible determinants of a firm's share price.

Q4 State one benefit of being a company as compared to being a sole trader.

ANSWERS

a business that is owned by shareholders but whose shares may not be advertised

A1 false; owners can be outside investors and do not have to be family members (although they may be)

A2 to vote; to receive dividends; to benefit from an increase in share price

A3 likely dividends; likely profits; the expected value of the company

A4 limited liability — investors cannot lose their own personal assets

***examiner's* note** The value of forming a company depends on whether the owners need to protect themselves with limited liability, on whether people believe a company has more status than a sole trader, and on the way earnings of individuals and companies are taxed. Private limited companies can place restrictions on the sale of their shares. This means they can be safer from hostile takeovers than plcs, which cannot control whom shares are sold to.

Limited liability

Q1 The opposite of limited liability is known as u................ l................

Q2 Which of the following types of organisation has/have limited liability: (a) Ltd; (b) plc; (c) sole trader?

Q3 How might limited liability benefit an organisation?

Q4 Mary invested £300 in a company. The company has since been liquidated. Has Mary lost all of her £300?

ANSWERS

investors can only lose the amount they have invested; their personal possessions are safe

A1 unlimited liability

A2 (a) and (b) — investors in these are protected, but sole traders can lose their personal possessions

A3 may help attract investors because there is a limit to what they can lose

A4 she might have — it depends on the extent to which the sale of the firm's assets can meet its liabilities

examiner's note The need for limited liability depends on the need to attract investors and the risk of losing your personal possessions. However, with the right of limited liability comes the obligation to reveal more information to investors, e.g. by registering company accounts. Some firms do not want to disclose too much information and so prefer to remain private limited companies — these have to publish fewer financial data than plcs.

Sources of finance

Q1 State two external sources of finance.

Q2 State two internal sources of finance.

Q3 What might a bank take into account before giving a firm a loan?

Q4 What determines the best form of finance for a firm?

ANSWERS

the ways in which a firm can raise money

A1 debentures; loans; shares

A2 asset sales (e.g. land and stocks); retained profits

A3 collateral; risk; experience; plans

A4 interest rates; repayment terms; desire to keep control
(willingness to let others vote); whether finance is needed in the
short term or long term

***examiner's* note** Short-term sources of finance include creditors and an
overdraft. Long-term sources include issued share capital and loans.

The ability of a firm to sell shares depends on the price, the returns available
elsewhere and the expected dividends and share price movements.

Internal sources of finance

Q1 Why might a firm be reluctant to issue more shares?

Q2 Why might a company want to change from a public limited company to a private limited company?

Q3 Distinguish between a loan and an overdraft.

ANSWERS

ways of raising money from within the business

A1 loss of control; existing owners may want to retain control of the shares and not bring in more owners for fear of objective clashes

A2 to reduce fear of takeover; to reduce conflict of objectives

A3 a loan is a fixed-term form of borrowing; an overdraft is a short-term form and can be called in at any time

***examiner's* note** Internal finance usually involves slower growth than raising money externally. Relying on internal sources may mean that a firm misses out on expansion opportunities.

The extent of borrowing that a firm has will depend on interest rates, what it intends to invest in and the expected returns on its projects.

Ordinary shares

Q1 Every year a company may pay a reward called a d................. to its shareholders out of profits. What might determine its size?

Q2 A company must pay money to its shareholders each year. True or false? Explain.

Q3 State two reasons why someone might buy a share.

Q4 All shareholders have one vote each. True or false? Explain.

ANSWERS

A1 dividend; the size of profits, what others pay and the share price

A2 false; it depends on the shareholders' wishes

A3 • to receive dividends
    • to gain from the share price increasing
    • to vote

A4 false; one vote per share

examiner's note Share capital represents one form of long-term finance; others include loans and debentures.

A firm is less likely to raise funds by selling shares if the existing owners do not want to lose control and existing borrowing is very low so that more loans are possible.

Venture capital

Q1 You need a known amount of money for a fixed period of time. Which is the best way of raising finance: a loan, an overdraft or share capital?

Q2 You may need some money in the next 12 months but you are not sure it will be needed. Should you obtain it through a loan, an overdraft or share capital?

Q3 An ordinary shareholder receives one vote regardless of the number of shares owned. True or false?

Q4 What is the interest rate?

ANSWERS

A1 loan

A2 overdraft

A3 false; one vote per share

A4 the cost of borrowing money; the amount paid on borrowed money; it is also the reward paid to savers

examiner's note A big question facing some entrepreneurs is whether they want to share control of their business. Selling shares may bring in useful finance but it does mean there are new owners.

Employee

Q1 State two reasons why an entrepreneur might recruit staff.

Q2 State two factors an entrepreneur might consider when employing someone.

Q3 State two responsibilities of an employer to an employee.

Q4 State two problems of hiring people for a small business.

ANSWERS

someone who works for the business

A1 to get extra help; to get specialist knowledge and skills

A2 costs; skills and qualifications; ease of working with them

A3 to provide a contract; to pay as agreed; to provide a safe working environment; not to discriminate

A4 may not enjoy working with them; they increase costs; they need managing, which takes time

***examiner's* note** Hiring an employee can be a big commitment — it increases costs and he or she needs to be managed properly.

Temporary employees

Q1 Why might a business use temporary staff?

Q2 What is meant by part-time staff?

Q3 Why might a business use part-time staff?

Q4 What is a salary?

ANSWERS

employees hired for a specific period of time

A1 because of seasonal changes or a new one-off contract

A2 employees who work less than full-time hours

A3 because it is busy at certain times of day or on certain days

A4 the annual earnings of an employee, usually paid in monthly instalments

***examiner's* note** Managers will want to match the supply to demand; if demand increases, managers want to be able to supply more and if demand falls, they will want to reduce supply. Temporary labour helps them achieve this.

Management consultants

Q1 Which of the following is not an external source of advice: banks, accountants, employees, consultants?

Q2 Why might a business want to employ a consultant?

Q3 What might be a disadvantage of employing a consultant?

ANSWERS

specialists employed to advise the business

A1 employees

A2 for specialist advice; to help ensure all legal requirements are met

A3 the cost

***examiner's* note** Employing management consultants can be useful but they can be expensive and they do not necessarily know your business as well as you do.

Variable and fixed costs

Q1 What is the equation to calculate break-even output?

Q2 Sales price £50; variable cost per unit £20; fixed costs £6,000. What is the profit or loss at 300 units?

Q3 State three assumptions of simple break-even analysis.

Q4 Selling price £20; variable cost per unit £5; break-even output 200 units. What are the fixed costs?

ANSWERS

costs that change and costs that do not change with output

A1 break-even output = $\dfrac{\text{fixed costs}}{\text{contribution per unit}}$

A2 profit = contribution − fixed costs: £9,000 − £6,000 = £3,000

A3 • all items are sold at the same price
   • all items produced are sold
   • the variable cost per unit is constant

A4 contribution per unit = £20 − £5 = £15. If break-even output is 200 units, fixed costs must be 200 × £15 = £3,000.

***examiner's* note** The need to control costs is especially important if there is a high degree of competition, profit margins are small and customers can easily switch to competitors' products if the firm's prices are too high.

Cutting the variable costs per unit means fewer units have to be sold to break even. However, this may mean quality suffers due to cheaper inputs and so the firm struggles to sell this number and therefore makes a loss.

 **43 ANSWERS**

Total costs

Q1 Total revenue – total costs = ...

Q2 Cost per unit £4; number of units sold 400. What are total costs?

Q3 Fixed costs £4,000; variable costs £5 per unit; sales 200 units. What are total costs?

Q4 How can profits increase if total costs have increased?

ANSWERS

A1 profit

A2 total costs = £4 × 400 = £1,600

A3 variable costs = £5 × 200 = £1,000
total costs = £4,000 + £1,000 = £5,000

A4 if revenue increases by more, e.g. more sales or a higher price

***examiner's* note** Whether a cut in costs leads to an increase in profits depends on what is happening to total revenue. Reducing costs may not increase profits if, for example, the quality of the products falls, leading to lower sales.

Total revenue

Q1 Total revenue £6,000; sales 300 units. What is the unit price?

Q2 Total revenue £4,000 per week; selling price £50. How many units are sold per week?

Q3 If demand is price inelastic and the price is increased, will total revenue increase or decrease? Why?

Q4 Profit £20,000; total costs £12,000. What is total revenue?

ANSWERS ▶▶

A1 $\dfrac{\pounds 6,000}{300} = \pounds 20$

A2 $\dfrac{\pounds 4,000}{\pounds 50} = 80$ units

A3 increase; the fall in quantity demanded as a percentage will be less than the percentage increase in price

A4 £32,000

***examiner's* note** Whether a price increase leads to an increase or decrease in total revenue depends on the price elasticity of demand; revenue will decrease when price increases if demand is price elastic. Simply increasing revenue does not guarantee that profits will increase, because costs may have increased even more (e.g. to promote the products).

Profit

Q1 What is meant by retained profit?

Q2 State three non-financial measures of a firm's efficiency.

Q3 Why is profit important to a business?

Q4 Distinguish between 'cash in' and 'revenue'.

ANSWERS

turnover minus costs

A1 profit kept within a business as opposed to being paid out as dividends

A2 proportion of inputs recycled; emission levels; wastage and scrap rates

A3 for investment and to reward owners

A4 cash in is actual tangible money received, while revenue is the value of sales — a credit sale generates revenue, not cash in

***examiner's* note** If firms make a profit, the directors must decide what to do with this. They may retain the profit in the business or pay it out as dividends. The extent to which a firm retains its profits rather than pays them out depends on the need to boost the share price and reward the firm's owners, as compared to the need to retain funds for future investment.

 **ANSWERS**

Break-even output

Q1 What is the equation to calculate break-even output?

Q2 Sales price £20; variable costs per unit £15; fixed costs £1,000. What is the break-even output?

Q3 Would an increase in fixed costs increase or decrease the break-even output? Explain.

Q4 Will an increase in price shift the total cost line? Explain.

ANSWERS

the minimum level of output at which total revenue equals total costs

A1 break-even output = $\dfrac{\text{fixed costs}}{\text{contribution per unit}}$

A2 contribution per unit = £20 − £15 = £5

break-even output = $\dfrac{£1,000}{£5}$ = 200 units

A3 increase; need to sell more to cover higher costs

A4 no; it does not affect costs — it will cause the total revenue curve to pivot upwards

***examiner's* note** Break-even analysis can help a firm to make decisions about pricing, changing costs and changing output. The value of break-even analysis depends on how reliable the estimates of sales, costs and revenues are. It can help a firm to plan, provided the underlying assumptions are valid.

Contribution per unit

Q1 Selling price £40; variable costs per unit £25; fixed costs £2,000. What is the contribution per unit?

Q2 Contribution per unit £20; variable costs per unit £40. What is the selling price?

Q3 Selling price £30; variable costs per unit £5; fixed costs £5,000. What is the break-even output?

Q4 The lower the contribution per unit, the greater the break-even output. True or false? Explain.

ANSWERS ▶▶

selling price minus variable cost per unit

A1 £40 – £25 = £15

A2 £60

A3 contribution per unit = £30 – £5 = £25

break-even output = $\dfrac{£5,000}{£25}$ = 200 units

A4 true; more units need to be sold to cover the fixed costs

examiner's **note** Contribution per unit will be higher if a firm can reduce
the material or labour costs per unit or if it can increase the price per unit.

Total contribution

Q1 Is rent a fixed or variable cost? Why?

Q2 Fixed costs never change. True or false? Explain.

Q3 A coffee shop sells drinks for £2. The variable costs are £0.50. What is the total contribution if 500 cups of coffee are sold?

ANSWERS

revenue minus variable costs

A1 fixed; because it does not change with output

A2 false; they do not change with output but they can change for other reasons, e.g. rent

A3 contribution per unit = £1.50

total contribution = £1.50 × 500 = £750

***examiner's* note** Total contribution from an order = contribution per unit × the number of units. Profit = total contribution – fixed costs. On financial grounds, the best order to accept is the one with the highest contribution to fixed costs. Any order that has a positive contribution is helping to pay off fixed costs; even if a loss is made overall, this may be smaller than the loss would have been if the order had not been accepted.

Margin of safety

Q1 What is the equation to calculate the margin of safety?

Q2 Present output 300 units; unit price £20; variable costs per unit £15; fixed costs £1,000. What is the margin of safety?

Q3 Will an increase in price decrease the break-even output? Explain.

Q4 Will a decrease in variable costs increase or decrease the break-even output? Explain.

ANSWERS

A1 margin of safety = output – break-even output

A2 break-even output = $\dfrac{£1,000}{£5}$ = 200 units
   margin of safety = 300 – 200 = 100 units

A3 yes; fewer units need to be sold to cover total costs

A4 decrease; fewer units need to be sold to cover fixed costs

***examiner's* note** Using break-even analysis through a number of 'what if?' scenarios (e.g. 'What level of output and sales will be needed to break even even if we sell at a price of £x per unit?') can help entrepreneurs decide whether it is likely to be profitable to supply a product at a certain price or to start production.

Cash flow

Q1 Why is cash flow important?

Q2 How can a business make a profit but have negative cash flow?

Q3 Materials and labour are used and paid for in cash and cost £200; the products are then sold on credit for £300. What are the cash flow and the profit position of the business?

Q4 What is a cash-flow forecast?

ANSWERS

the movement of cash into and out of a business

A1 cash flow is needed for liquidity; to pay the bills

A2 if it sells on credit, this is counted as revenue but the cash is not paid yet

A3 cash flow = cash in − cash out = £0 − £200 = (£200)

profit = revenue − costs = £300 − £200 = £100

A4 a forecast of future inflows and outflows of money

***examiner's* note** Cash is essential to survival; without it you cannot pay your bills and will have to close down. Managing the timings of cash coming in and out is very important.

Cash-flow forecast

Q1 State one disadvantage of holding high levels of cash.

Q2 State two ways of increasing cash flow.

Q3 State two reasons why cash outflow might be higher than expected.

Q4 State two reasons why cash inflow may be lower than expected.

ANSWERS

A1 opportunity cost — the money could be invested elsewhere

A2 overdraft; loan; chase debtors; delay paying suppliers

A3 interest rates go up; suppliers put up prices; suppliers demand payment more quickly

A4 lower sales than forecast; customers slow to pay

***examiner's* note** A cash-flow forecast is an important part of financial planning. Managers can identify when extra cash will be needed or when too much cash is sitting idle. The value of a cash-flow forecast depends on the accuracy of the planning, i.e. the extent to which the manager correctly anticipates future inflows and outflows and then takes appropriate action.

Improving cash flow

Q1 What is a loan?

Q2 What is meant by the sale of assets?

Q3 What is meant by factoring?

Q4 Delaying payment to suppliers improves cash flow, but state one possible problem with this.

ANSWERS

improving the amount of cash coming into the business relative to the amount of cash leaving it

A1 borrowing for a fixed period of time at a set rate

A2 selling items owned by the business to raise cash, e.g. stocks, land, buildings

A3 when you sell items on credit, the factor pays you the money owed (minus a fee); the customer then pays the factor later

A4 may lose the goodwill of suppliers; suppliers may not worry so much about quality; they may not prioritise your orders in future

***examiner's* note** You need to think carefully about the best method of improving cash flow, e.g. chasing customers for payment may lose their goodwill but this may not matter if your product is in huge demand; an overdraft may be better than a loan if you are not sure whether you will need the money or not.

Budgeting

Q1 State two possible benefits of budgeting.

Q2 State one way in which IT can benefit the budgeting process.

Q3 State two possible problems of budgeting.

Q4 State three ways in which a budget might be set.

ANSWERS

a system of setting and monitoring future financial targets

A1 • may motivate by setting targets
   • coordinates
   • mechanism of control

A2 easier to update/monitor budgets, e.g. using spreadsheets

A3 superiors and subordinates may disagree over the targets; problems estimating future costs

A4 based on past figures; based on competitors; based on objectives

examiner's **note** A budget is a means of controlling spending, coordinating activities, motivating staff and agreeing plans. The value of budgeting depends on the way in which budgets are set (e.g. are they agreed or imposed?) and the levels at which they are set.

Adverse expenditure variance

Q1 What is a budget?

Q2 State two reasons why subordinates may resist a budget.

Q3 If the budgeted revenue is £10,000 and the actual revenue is £8,000, this is adverse variance. True or false?

ANSWERS

A1 a future financial target for revenue or expenditure

A2 may think it is too low; may think it restricts their actions; do not want to have to account for their decisions; do not like planning

A3 true; profits are lower than expected

***examiner's* note** Even if the variance is positive, it could be of concern to managers. Why did they not anticipate the higher revenue or lower costs? Is there anything they can learn from this for next time?

Variance analysis

Q1 What is a 'favourable' variance?

Q2 Budgeted turnover £8,000; actual turnover £10,000. State the variance and whether it is adverse or favourable.

Q3 If the budgeted costs are higher than the actual costs, is this a favourable or adverse variance? Explain.

Q4 If the budgeted revenue is higher than the actual revenue, is this a favourable or adverse variance? Explain.

ANSWERS

A1 occurs when actual profits are more than budgeted, e.g. costs are lower than budgeted and/or revenues are greater than budgeted

A2 £2,000 favourable

A3 favourable; profits will be higher than expected on this basis

A4 adverse; profits will be lower than expected on this basis

examiner's **note** The extent to which a variance causes concern depends on whether it is favourable or adverse, how big the variance is, and whether the managers can work out why it occurred and learn from this.

Profit and loss

Q1 Why might an entrepreneur want to earn profit?

Q2 If the revenue of a business is £200,000 and the costs are £220,000, has the business made a profit or a loss this year?

Q3 All profits are paid out to the shareholders each year. True or false?

Q4 If revenues are higher than expected, the profits are higher as well. True or false?

ANSWERS

A1 to finance investment; to pay out as a reward to the owners

A2 it has made a loss

A3 false; they can be retained in the business

A4 false; costs may be higher as well

examiner's note Many start ups make a loss in the first year or so because of the set-up costs and because demand takes time to build. A business cannot make a loss forever, but it is not unusual to make a loss in the early years.

Profitability

Q1 Sales are £2,000; profits are £400. What is the profit margin?

Q2 Is a high profit margin always good? Explain.

Q3 Capital invested is £400,000; profit is £20,000. What is the return on capital?

Q4 A large profit could be a small return on capital. True or false?

ANSWERS

A1 $\dfrac{\text{profit}}{\text{sales}} \times 100 = \dfrac{£400}{£2,000} \times 100 = 20\%$

A2 no; your overall return (the return on capital) depends on how many units you sell as well as the profit margin

A3 $\dfrac{\text{profit}}{\text{capital}} \times 100 = \dfrac{£20,000}{£400,000} \times 100 = 5\%$

A4 true — if you have invested large sums of money into the business, the profit may be a small return

***examiner's* note** Remember the difference between profit and profitability: profit is a number measured in pounds; profitability is a percentage.

Improving profitability

Q1 How is profitability measured?

Q2 State two ways of increasing the profit margin.

Q3 How can marketing affect profitability?

Q4 How can operations affect profitability?

ANSWERS

A1 using the profit margin and return on capital; as a percentage

A2 increasing price; reducing the unit costs

A3 influences the level of sales and the price that can be charged

A4 influence the unit costs and the number that can be bought and sold

***examiner's* note** Increasing profitability can involve all the functions of the business: human resources can affect the productivity of staff; marketing can affect sales; operations can affect unit costs; and finance can affect whether funds are used efficiently.

Organisational structure

Q1 What is meant by the span of control?

Q2 What is a functional structure?

Q3 What is a matrix structure?

Q4 State two reasons why an effective organisational structure is important.

ANSWERS

the way in which jobs are organised (e.g. who reports to whom)

A1 the number of employees reporting directly to a superior

A2 an approach where jobs are grouped according to their function

A3 an approach that cuts across traditional functions and in which individuals report to more than one boss

A4
• affects the speed of decision making and efficiency
• can affect the quality of service provided

***examiner's* note** Organisational structure involves decisions regarding job design, levels of hierarchy, span of control and the grouping of jobs. The structure may need to change as the organisation grows. Organisational structure can help a firm to be more competitive, but success also depends on the product itself, the marketing and the way the product or service is produced.

Span of control

Q1 If the span of control is widened, is the number of levels of hierarchy likely to increase or decrease? Explain.

Q2 For managers wanting to keep tight control, is the span of control likely to be narrow or wide? Why?

Q3 State two possible benefits of a narrow span of control.

Q4 State two possible disadvantages of a narrow span of control.

ANSWERS ▶▶

the number of subordinates directly responsible to a superior

A1 decrease; fewer levels of managers are needed

A2 narrow; because this means there are relatively few people to monitor

A3
- may mean superiors keep a tight control over subordinates
- may lead to greater hierarchy and opportunities for promotion

A4
- may mean subordinates feel too controlled and become demotivated because they lack independence
- may lead to many levels of hierarchy, causing communication problems from the top to the bottom

examiner's **note** There is no correct span of control — it depends on a range of factors, e.g. the task, the subordinates and the superior. The span of control is likely to be wider if subordinates are skilled and trusted to do the job, and managers are prepared to delegate.

 ANSWERS

Levels of hierarchy

Q1 Is a narrower span of control likely to increase or decrease the number of levels of hierarchy? Why?

Q2 Is the span of control likely to be wider or narrower if the manager trusts employees to do the job well? Why?

Q3 State two possible advantages to an organisation of having many levels of hierarchy.

Q4 State one possible problem of having many levels of hierarchy.

ANSWERS

layers of authority within an organisation

A1 increase; fewer subordinates are supervised by each manager, so more managers are needed, leading to more levels of hierarchy

A2 wider; the manager will not feel it necessary to have as close control

A3 • creates promotion opportunities
   • may mean narrower spans of control and so more control over activities

A4 may lead to poor communication from top to bottom

***examiner's* note** The right organisational structure is important. It can affect costs, the speed of decision making and employees' motivation.

The 'correct' number of levels of hierarchy depends on the skills and attitudes of employees and managers, the nature of their tasks and the quality of communication.

Director

Q1 What does a manager do?

Q2 Who does a manager report to?

Q3 Who does a supervisor report to?

Q4 What is meant by 'job allocation'?

 ANSWERS

appointed by shareholders to oversee
the management of the business

A1 plans, organises, coordinates and controls

A2 the directors

A3 the managers

A4 it determines who is responsible for different tasks

examiner's **note** Directors are appointed by shareholders to be their
'watchdog' and monitor the actions of managers. Sometimes managers may
pursue their own objectives, which may not match shareholders' objectives, so
managers need monitoring.

Labour turnover

Q1 What is the equation for labour turnover?

Q2 State two possible causes of high labour turnover.

Q3 State two problems of high labour turnover.

ANSWERS

the proportion of employees leaving a business over a period of time

A1 labour turnover (%) = $\dfrac{\text{no. of employees leaving a business over given period}}{\text{average number employed}} \times 100$

A2 poor pay; poor conditions; poor management

A3 recruitment costs; training costs; disruptive for staff

***examiner's* note** Labour turnover is one indicator of the effectiveness of human resource management. Others include productivity and absenteeism. The level of labour turnover varies from industry to industry (e.g. the fast-food industry typically employs students and seasonal workers, and so has a high labour turnover).

Labour productivity

Q1 If labour productivity increases, output also increases.
True or false?

Q2 An increase in labour productivity leads to an increase in sales.
True or false?

Q3 State two ways of increasing labour productivity.

Q4 State two benefits of higher labour productivity.

ANSWERS

the output per worker

A1 false; with fewer workers the output per worker may be higher, but the total output may be the same or even lower

A2 false; the firm may produce output but not be able to sell it

A3 training; improved working practices; better technology

A4 • may reduce the labour costs per unit
• may increase output

***examiner's* note** Employees may resist attempts to increase productivity if they think it will lead to redundancies — if individuals produce more, a firm may be able to lose some of them. Efforts to increase productivity are likely to be more successful if employees see the need, if they are involved in the changes, if jobs are not lost and if they gain extra rewards as a result.

Recruitment

Q1 State the difference between internal recruitment and external recruitment.

Q2 When recruiting externally, how might a firm advertise the job?

Q3 State two possible benefits to a firm of internal recruitment compared to external recruitment.

Q4 Recruitment attracts applicants; the firm must then choose between these different people. This is the s................ process.

ANSWERS

activities involved in attracting applicants for a job vacancy

A1 internal recruitment involves looking to fill the vacancy from applicants already working for the business; external recruitment attracts applicants from outside the organisation

A2 newspapers (local/national); internet; magazines; employment agencies

A3 • may be quicker
   • may be cheaper than advertising externally

A4 selection

***examiner's* note** Hiring an employee is making an investment. Getting it right is important; otherwise they may leave and the firm has to start recruiting again, or they stay but do not do the job well. The amount spent on recruitment depends on the resources of the firm, how important the job is and the state of the labour market.

 **ANSWERS**

Selection

Q1 How could you measure the effectiveness of the selection process?

Q2 State two ways in which a firm might select an employee.

Q3 State two possible problems if the wrong people are selected for a job.

Q4 If someone is asked to leave their job, this is known as d........................ Give one reason for this.

ANSWERS

A1 how long did it take? how much did it cost? was the right person chosen? how long did the person stay?

A2
- by interview
- by testing, e.g. IQ test

A3
- they may leave and you need to recruit again
- they may not be very productive

A4 dismissal; they cannot do their job properly

***examiner's* note** The retention rate measures how long people stay with a firm once they have been recruited. If the retention rate is low, it may suggest the selection process is poor — the people selected leave the business relatively quickly. The amount of time and money likely to be spent on selection depends on the importance of the job and the risks involved in choosing the wrong person.

Person specification

Q1 State two elements of a job description.

Q2 State two elements of a person specification.

Q3 State two ways of selecting staff.

Q4 What is a CV?

ANSWERS))

A1 job title; duties and responsibilities; reporting relationships

A2 skills; experience; qualifications

A3 interview; CV; tests

A4 curriculum vitae — a document sent in by someone applying for a job providing information about themselves such as their personal details, education and work experience

***examiner's* note** Recruiting someone externally may provide more choice but may take longer and be more expensive.

On-the-job training

Q1 What is the opposite of on-the-job training? Define this.

Q2 Training that occurs when an employee first joins an organisation is called i.......................... training. What might this involve?

Q3 State three possible benefits of greater training.

Q4 Why might a firm not invest in training?

ANSWERS

efforts to increase the knowledge and skills of individuals while they undertake the work itself

A1 off-the-job training; training undertaken away from the actual work itself

A2 induction; introduction to the job, colleagues and the business

A3 • more motivated employees
• more skilled employees
• leads to higher productivity, better quality and lower unit costs

A4 not needed — employees have the necessary skills already; the firm does not have the funds; managers do not see the need

***examiner's* note** Training is an investment; it should be undertaken only if the benefits exceed the costs. The value of training depends on how much it costs, the extent to which employees develop new skills and understanding, and the impact on business performance.

 69 **ANSWERS**

Job design

Q1 What is job enrichment?

Q2 What is job enlargement?

Q3 What makes a well-designed job?

Q4 Why does job design matter?

ANSWERS

the responsibilities, resources and tasks that are included in a job

A1 providing more challenging tasks and responsibilities as part of a job — this is called 'vertical loading'

A2 adding more tasks of a similar level of responsibility — this is called 'horizontal loading'

A3 depends on the variety of tasks, the level of feedback, the significance of tasks and the extent to which employees see the point of their job

A4 affects motivation and therefore productivity and labour turnover

***examiner's* note** According to Herzberg, job design is key to motivation; the job provides intrinsic motivators which mean people want to come to work.

 70 **ANSWERS**

Teamwork

Q1 Teamwork can help meet employees' social needs. These were identified in M............ hierarchy of needs. What were the others?

Q2 Teamwork is often linked to attempts to make individuals responsible for their work and reduce waste. This is known as e............

Q3 State two benefits of teamwork.

Q4 State two problems of teamwork.

ANSWERS

A1 Maslow's; physiological, security, ego and self-actualisation

A2 empowerment

A3 • motivates staff
• employees share skills, which may lead to better problem solving

A4 • some individuals may prefer working alone
• some may not contribute fully, leading to problems
• group norms may be poor

***examiner's* note** More firms are encouraging teamwork as a way of fulfilling social needs and delegating decisions to employees. The value of teamwork depends on the extent to which skills are shared, the reaction of employees involved and the ability of employees to work together.

Empowerment

Q1 Empowerment may give employees greater challenge in their work. According to Herzberg, this can lead to job e............................

Q2 Is empowerment most likely to be associated with physiological or self-actualisation needs? Why?

Q3 State two possible benefits to a firm of empowerment.

Q4 State two reasons why employees might resist attempts to empower them.

ANSWERS ▶▶

A1 enrichment

A2 self-actualisation; it involves exercising greater authority

A3 • may motivate employees by giving them greater authority
  • may lead to better decisions and more efficient processes, as those who make the decisions are those who do the work

A4 • may feel it is a form of exploitation
  • may not want greater authority

***examiner's* note** Empowerment is more likely if employees are trained and skilled, and if managers are willing to delegate. Some employees will welcome the opportunity to have more control over their work; others will not be interested and resent the extra effort and work involved.

Motivation

Q1 Which theorist highlighted the difference between hygiene factors and motivators? Explain the difference.

Q2 State the different levels in Maslow's hierarchy of needs from lowest to highest.

Q3 State four factors relating to the design of a job that might make it motivating.

Q4 How can motivation affect employees' performance?

ANSWERS

when individuals want to do something for themselves

A1 Herzberg; hygiene factors prevent dissatisfaction, while motivators satisfy

A2 physiological, security, social, ego, self-actualisation

A3
- task variety
- authority
- challenge
- sense of a complete task

A4 might lead to better attendance, fewer mistakes, better-quality work

***examiner's* note** Motivation does not guarantee better performance. Performance also relies on technology, the equipment used, skills and working practices.

Money may influence employees' motivation, but motivation is also likely to depend on factors such as job design, feedback, the opportunity for advancement and level of responsibility.

 **ANSWERS**

Maslow's hierarchy of needs

Q1 Offering pensions to employees is aimed at meeting their s.............. needs. Explain your answer.

Q2 Giving employees authority to make decisions for themselves is aimed at which level of needs? Explain.

Q3 State two ways of satisfying employees' social needs.

Q4 State two ways in which a manager might satisfy employees' self-actualisation needs.

ANSWERS

physiological, safety (security), social, esteem (ego), self-actualisation

A1 security; they will have money when they retire

A2 self-actualisation; employees have more control over their own work and can show their abilities

A3 a listening approach; teamwork; company days out

A4 increased authority; greater variety in tasks at work

***examiner's* note** Maslow's work highlighted that individuals may be at different stages of the hierarchy of needs and that employees have many different needs. This means that managers may need to use a variety of rewards to motivate all their staff.

The power of money to motivate depends on which needs are unfulfilled (e.g. lower- or higher-level needs), how much is offered, what others are receiving, how much employees earn already and what the extra pay is linked to.

Herzberg's two factor theory

Q1 Hygiene factors are similar to the lower-level needs on Maslow's hierarchy. State the two lowest-level needs on this hierarchy.

Q2 According to Herzberg, you are either satisfied or dissatisfied at work. True or false? Explain.

Q3 Identify two hygiene factors.

Q4 Identify two motivators.

ANSWERS

identified hygiene factors, which prevent dissatisfaction, and motivators, which satisfy

A1 physiological needs and security needs

A2 false; you may be 'not dissatisfied'

A3
- working conditions
- company policy
- colleagues
- basic pay

A4
- promotion opportunities
- greater authority
- recognition for achievement
- challenge in the job

***examiner's* note** Whenever change is happening in the workplace, think of the impact on employees in terms of Herzberg's hygiene factors and motivators. According to Herzberg, managers are more likely to motivate their employees if they get the extrinsic factors at work right and focus on the intrinsic factors of the job itself.

Job enrichment

Q1 Job enrichment adds tasks with more authority; what is job enlargement?

Q2 According to Herzberg, is job enrichment a hygiene factor or a motivator? Why?

Q3 State two possible benefits of job enrichment.

Q4 Why might employees resist attempts to enrich their jobs?

ANSWERS

redesigning a job to make it more challenging and fulfilling, e.g. providing a greater degree of authority

A1 adds tasks with similar levels of authority

A2 a motivator because it provides more challenge and authority, and can therefore increase satisfaction

A3 • should motivate and may lead to higher productivity
• may mean employees need less supervision

A4 may distrust managers and think it is just a way of giving them extra work; may not want extra challenge

***examiner's* note** Intrinsic factors at work relate to the job itself. Extrinsic factors are factors associated with the work, such as pay and conditions. Job enrichment is concerned with intrinsic factors.

Managers are most likely to try to enrich jobs if they appreciate the importance of people to the success of the business.

(76) ANSWERS

Delegation

Q1 State two benefits of delegation.

Q2 State two problems of delegation.

Q3 State two reasons why managers may not want to delegate.

Q4 State two factors that may influence someone's decision to delegate.

ANSWERS

when a manager entrusts another employee with a task

A1
- reduces overload of superiors, allowing them to focus on strategy
- may make use of subordinates' skills
- may motivate subordinates

A2
- may lead to poorer decision making
- risky for managers because they lose control

A3
- may fear loss of control
- may not trust subordinates
- may want to keep certain decisions for themselves

A4
- skill of subordinate
- degree of risk
- willingness to give up control

***examiner's* note** The effectiveness of delegation depends on whether subordinates have the correct information, sufficient resources and appropriate standards. Some tasks may not be suitable to delegate.

 **ANSWERS**

Operations management

Q1 What is meant by productivity?

Q2 What is meant by 'capacity utilisation of 70%'?

Q3 If the unit cost is £5 and output is 40 units, what are the total costs?

Q4 What effect does the under-utilisation of capacity have on unit costs?

ANSWERS

A1 the output produced in relation to the inputs used, e.g. the output per hour or per employee

A2 the present output is 70% of the maximum output

A3 £200

A4 low capacity utilisation means the unit costs increase as the fixed costs are spread over fewer units

***examiner's* note** The way operations are managed has a big effect on the cost per unit, the number that can be produced and the quality of the process.

Capacity

Q1 If a firm is capable of producing 200 units but is producing only 40 units at the moment, what is its capacity utilisation (%)?

Q2 A firm is producing 200 units and is operating at 20% capacity utilisation. What number of units is full capacity?

Q3 State two ways in which a firm might increase its capacity.

Q4 State two ways in which a firm might react if demand is too high for its existing capacity.

ANSWERS

measures the maximum output that a firm can produce given its existing resources

A1 $\frac{40}{200} \times 100 = 20\%$

A2 $20\% = 200 \implies 1\% = 10 \implies 100\%$ (i.e. full capacity) $= 1,000$ units

A3 • increase investment in training
   • increase investment in capital equipment and technology

A4 • try to increase capacity (but this takes time)
   • increase prices
   • start a waiting list

***examiner's* note** Simply having the capacity to produce does not guarantee sales — this depends on the level of demand. Capacity can act as a constraint on a business — it limits its output (and therefore sales). Remember it can take time to change capacity, e.g. to install new equipment.

(**79**) **ANSWERS**

Under-utilisation of capacity

Q1 If a firm is able to produce 200 units a day but it is actually producing 120 units a day, what is its capacity utilisation (%)?

Q2 When firms operate under capacity, is the unit cost likely to be high or low? Why?

Q3 State why a firm might be operating under capacity.

Q4 State two ways in which a firm may react if it is operating under capacity.

ANSWERS

occurs when a firm is producing
below the maximum it could produce
given existing resources

A1 $\dfrac{120}{200} \times 100 = 60\%$

A2 high; the fixed costs per unit are spread over fewer units

A3 sales may have fallen (e.g. due to competitors entering the market) or the product may still be in the 'introduction' phase

A4 • may try to boost demand or produce for other firms
• may reduce its capacity

examiner's note To boost capacity utilisation, a firm may undertake more marketing activities, e.g. greater promotion. However, this costs money and the firm will have to ensure that the benefits cover this.

The impact of operating below capacity depends on the level of short-fall, how long the situation is expected to last and the effect on unit costs.

Non-standard orders

Q1 State two ways a business can match production to an increase in demand.

Q2 What are different types of stocks?

Q3 State two reasons for holding stocks.

Q4 State two benefits of subcontracting.

ANSWERS ▶▶

unusual changes in demand

A1 changing stock levels; temporary staff; part-time staff

A2 materials; works in progress; finished goods

A3 to meet demand; just in case supplies do not turn up

A4 to meet high levels of demand; to use specialist skills

***examiner's* note** Demand for some products may fluctuate a great deal, e.g. demand for umbrellas, sun cream, de-icer and road-side assistance varies with the weather.

Quality

Q1 State two reasons why good quality matters.

Q2 State two reasons why quality may be poor.

Q3 How can money be saved by improving quality?

Q4 Better quality may make demand price inelastic. Explain what this means.

ANSWERS

A1 generates customer goodwill and repeat business; may differentiate the business and allow higher prices

A2 lack of training; lack of investment; use of cheap materials; lack of understanding of what the customer wants

A3 there may be less waste; fewer rejects; fewer returned items

A4 demand becomes less sensitive to price (the change in quantity demanded is proportionately less than the change in price)

***examiner's* note** The need to improve quality is greater when competition increases because you must be better to stay ahead.

Quality assurance

Q1 The quality of a product depends on the extent to which it meets c_____ requirements.

Q2 When a firm inspects items to check for defects, this is known as q_____ c_____ Give one benefit of this.

Q3 State two ways in which a firm might improve its quality.

Q4 State two possible problems a firm might experience when trying to increase its quality.

ANSWERS ▶▶

activities undertaken to ensure that the quality of a good or service is maintained

A1 customer (or consumer)

A2 quality control; benefits include fewer mistakes, less wastage and fewer returned goods

A3 • by training its staff, so that fewer mistakes are made
    • by using better-quality supplies and materials

A4 • may require more investment, e.g. in inspection equipment
    • employees may resist changes in their working practices

***examiner's* note** The need for better quality is greater nowadays because of fiercer competition. As other firms improve their quality, it is important for any business to do the same in order to compete.

Better quality may help a firm succeed, but success also depends on factors such as marketing and competitors' actions.

 83 **ANSWERS**

Quality control

Q1 What is quality assurance?

Q2 What is TQM?

Q3 State two possible costs involved in improving quality.

Q4 State two ways in which better quality reduces costs.

ANSWERS

aims to find defects through a process of inspection

A1 aims to improve quality through a process that prevents errors from occurring

A2 total quality management — all employees are involved in improving quality

A3 training costs; costs of better inputs; costs of sampling and testing

A4 fewer errors to fix; fewer returned items; fewer dissatisfied customers wanting compensation

***examiner's* note** Improving quality can reduce costs and improve customer satisfaction. It should involve all employees to help prevent, and if necessary find, errors.

Customer service

Q1 State two reasons why good customer service matters.

Q2 State two ways of measuring the quality of customer service.

Q3 State two ways of improving customer service.

Q4 What is meant by 'falling market share'?

ANSWERS

the provision of service to customers before, during and after a purchase

A1 affects sales and customer loyalty; affects the competitiveness of the business

A2 using customer surveys; mystery visitors; monitoring repeat sales

A3 training; ensuring customer requirements are understood

A4 sales, as a percentage of the total market sales, are falling

***examiner's* note** Customer service can help a business to differentiate what it does and therefore make demand more price inelastic.

Technology

Q1 State two benefits of using better technology in operations.

Q2 State two factors to consider before choosing new technology.

Q3 What is the equation to calculate unit cost?

Q4 What is meant by productivity?

ANSWERS

A1 greater flexibility; more cost efficiency; higher productivity

A2 costs; flexibility; quality of output

A3 $\dfrac{\text{total cost}}{\text{output}}$

A4 output per input (e.g. output per worker)

***examiner's* note** The introduction of new technology often faces resistance because people are worried they will not know how to use it or they will lose their job or status.

Supplier

Q1 State two factors that influence the choice of a supplier.

Q2 State two ways in which suppliers influence the success of a business.

Q3 What is meant by 'capacity'?

Q4 What is meant by 'capacity utilisation of 12%'?

ANSWERS

A1 price; quality; reliability; capacity

A2 affect costs; can affect the quality and reliability of the final product; delays can halt production

A3 the maximum output of a business given a level of resources

A4 actual output is 12% of the maximum possible

***examiner's* note** If a business takes over its suppliers this is known as 'backward vertical integration'. If a supplier takes over the business it sells to, this is known as 'forward vertical integration'.

Business to business marketing (B2B)

Q1 What is marketing?

Q2 What two groups come together in a market?

Q3 State two possible features of B2B marketing.

Q4 What is B2C marketing?

ANSWERS

when businesses are selling to other businesses rather than the final customers

A1 the process of meeting customer needs in a mutually beneficial exchange process

A2 buyers and sellers

A3 professional buyer; relatively few customers; focused on performance

A4 business to customer (or consumer) marketing, e.g. selling to the final user

examiner's note Most marketing in an economy is actually business to business. In these cases, it is vital to understand how your work helps the other business to perform more effectively.

Mass marketing

Q1 Is mass marketing more or less likely than niche marketing to involve economies of scale? Why?

Q2 Outline a possible problem of mass marketing.

Q3 Is mass marketing likely to involve high or low fixed costs? Explain.

Q4 State two problems of niche marketing.

ANSWERS

when a product is aimed at the main segment of the market

A1 more; it involves large-scale sales

A2 it is likely to involve high investment in production processes; may not be flexible enough to individual customer needs

A3 high; it usually involves capital-intensive production processes

A4 limited market so profits may be low; vulnerable to losing customers as you are dependent on relatively few; threat of bigger firms entering the market

***examiner's* note** Mass marketing is easier in terms of production than competing in several different segments; a firm can produce a standardised product in volume. A mass marketing approach is likely to be adopted if there is a high level of demand for standardised products and if a firm is able to produce on a large scale.

 ANSWERS

Marketing mix

Q1 The marketing mix is sometimes described as the 4 Ps. What are these?

Q2 State three factors that might influence the price set for a product.

Q3 State two elements of the promotional mix.

Q4 State two factors that might influence the promotional spend.

ANSWERS

the combination of factors that influence a customer's decision to buy

A1 price, product, place (distribution) and promotion

A2 cost; level of demand; competitors' prices; price elasticity of demand; pricing strategy

A3 advertising; PR; merchandising; branding; sales promotion

A4 • promotional objectives
   • type of promotion used (e.g. advertising or public relations)

***examiner's* note** The marketing mix implements the strategy, which is derived from the objectives. The mix should be integrated, with the different elements complementing each other. The nature of the mix and the relative importance of its elements will vary according to the product and the strategy.

Distribution channels

Q1 A firm sells in 40 shops out of a possible 200. Its target is 50% of total outlets. How many more shops does it need to sell in?

Q2 State two factors a clothes manufacturer might consider when deciding which retailers to sell to.

Q3 State two ways in which effective distribution can affect a product's success.

Q4 Give two examples of a distribution target.

ANSWERS

A1 50% of 200 = 100, so the firm needs to sell in another 60 shops

A2 price offered; payment terms; how the clothes will be displayed and promoted in-store; impact on brand image

A3 • can make the product more available
    • can reduce costs (e.g. direct distribution)

A4 • to be sold in the northwest as well as the southeast
    • to be available in 80% of supermarket stores

***examiner's* note** Distribution is an important element of marketing; a firm is more likely to be successful if its distribution is low cost, enables quick delivery to the customer and provides easy access for customers. With the internet, the trend is for more direct distribution as customers buy direct from the manufacturer, e.g. Dell computers.

Price

Q1 A retailer buys items for £4 and adds on 25% to set the price. How much are they sold for?

Q2 The sensitivity of demand to price is measured by the .... of .... Give the equation.

Q3 State two reasons why a product's demand might not be very sensitive to price.

Q4 State two factors that might affect the price of a product.

ANSWERS ▶▶

A1 $\dfrac{25}{100} \times £4 = £1$ selling price = £4 + £1 = £5

A2 price elasticity of demand; $\dfrac{\text{\% change in quantity demanded}}{\text{\% change in price}}$

A3 heavy branding; relatively few substitutes; has a USP

A4 costs; demand; competitors' products; the rest of the mix

***examiner's* note** The price must be complemented by the other elements of the marketing mix, e.g. a high price fits with an exclusive product that has limited distribution and heavy promotion. Price may be particularly important when customers do not have much money, when there are many substitutes and when it is easy to compare prices with those of competitors.

Price elasticity of demand

Q1 If price elasticity of demand is −3, a 1% increase in price leads to a ....% reduction in quantity demanded.

Q2 If demand is price elastic, should the firm increase or decrease price to increase revenue? Explain.

Q3 If the price elasticity of demand is −3, is this elastic or inelastic? Why?

Q4 If sales rise by 5% when price falls by 10%, demand is price ....

ANSWERS

A1 3

A2 decrease; because of the relatively large increase in sales

A3 price elastic because the quantity demanded will change 3 times more than the change in price (in percentage terms)

A4 inelastic; the change in quantity demanded is less than the change in price — the value is −0.5

***examiner's* note** Demand for a product is likely to be more price elastic if there are several substitutes, brand loyalty is low and switching to alternatives is easy.

Remember that price elasticity shows how much quantity demanded changes in relation to price changes; income elasticity shows how much quantity demanded changes in relation to income. They are different!

 ANSWERS

Promotion

Q1 What is meant by advertising?

Q2 What is meant by merchandising?

Q3 What do the initials BOGOF stand for? Is it above- or below-the-line promotion?

Q4 State three factors that might determine how much a firm spends on promotion.

ANSWERS

A1 paid-for communications, such as print or TV adverts

A2 using the brand from one product to sell another, e.g. bands selling T-shirts with their names on them; merchandising can also refer to positioning, placement and promotion of products in stores

A3 buy one get one free; below-the-line promotion

A4 • overall resources available
  • marketing objectives
  • expected returns

***examiner's* note** There are many different forms of promotion. The most appropriate form depends on the type of product, the finance available and what the firm is trying to achieve. The effectiveness of a promotional campaign may depend on how much is invested in it, whether the right forms of promotion are chosen and what other firms are doing.

Public relations (PR)

Q1 How does advertising differ from public relations?

Q2 State two benefits for a company of good public relations.

Q3 PR is part of the p............................ mix.

Q4 PR is the responsibility of the operations function of a business. True or false?

activities to influence the public profile of an organisation

A1 unlike PR, advertising buys the media space and controls what is said

A2
- generates more sales and goodwill
- may boost share value
- brand loyalty
- brand awareness

A3 promotional

A4 false; it is the responsibility of the marketing function

***examiner's* note** The extent to which public relations matters depends on how effectively it is conducted and whether a firm's public profile is important. When a firm behaves ethically (i.e. does 'good' things, such as investing in the community), this may also be good for public relations. Some analysts believe that this is why some firms do it!

USP

Q1 If a firm has a technological USP, it may try to protect it legally with a p....................

Q2 Is developing a USP a method of delayering, differentiation or deforestation?

Q3 State two possible benefits of establishing a USP.

Q4 Is a USP likely to make demand more price elastic or inelastic? Explain.

ANSWERS

unique selling proposition (or point)

A1 patent

A2 differentiation

A3 • can charge higher prices
   • may enable higher profit margins

A4 price inelastic; customers will be less willing or able to switch

***examiner's* note** A USP may not last for ever; other firms may enter the market and imitate it. The value of a USP depends on how easy it is to protect against imitation, how much it meets customer needs and the extent to which customers are willing to pay for it.

Product portfolio analysis

Q1 A product with a large share of a slow-growth market is called a c............... c............... . What should be done with this product?

Q2 A product with a small share of a slow-growth market is called a d............... . What should be done with this product?

Q3 Explain what is meant by a 'star' product in the Boston Matrix.

Q4 Explain what is meant by a 'question mark' product in the Boston Matrix. What should be done with this product?

ANSWERS

shows the position of a firm's products in terms of market share and market growth

A1 cash cow; often used to finance new product development

A2 dog; either the product should be scrapped or money needs to be invested to revive it

A3 high market share in a fast-growth market

A4 small market share in a fast-growth market; investment needed to help it become a 'star' product

***examiner's* note** Portfolio analysis is part of the marketing planning process; firms analyse the existing position of products to plan what to do next.

The value of portfolio analysis depends on what decisions the manager takes as a result and whether the plans are implemented effectively.

 **ANSWERS**

Product life cycle

Q1 What labels are on the axes of the product life cycle diagram?

Q2 State the stages of the product life cycle.

Q3 Modifying a product to keep sales growing and prevent decline is known as an e................... s.................... Give two examples.

Q4 The B.............. M.............. provides an overview of the position of all the firm's products. State the four types of product that it shows.

ANSWERS

A1 time; sales

A2 introduction, growth, maturity, decline

A3 extension strategy; finding new uses for the product, finding new markets for the product

A4 Boston Matrix; dogs, cash cows, stars, problem children/ question marks

***examiner's* note** The product life cycle model may be of limited value. It is usually only clear afterwards what stage of the cycle a product was in before.

Research and development can produce new products to compensate for the fall in sales of existing products during the decline stage of their life cycle.

Competitiveness

Q1 How can market research help a business improve its competitiveness?

Q2 How can suppliers help a business improve its competitiveness?

Q3 How can employees help a business improve its competitiveness?

Q4 How can quality control help a business improve its competitiveness?

ANSWERS

the value your business provides to customers in relation to your rivals

A1 by gaining a better understanding of customer requirements so that the business can meet these needs more fully

A2 by enabling the business to charge a lower price or offer a faster or better-quality service

A3 through excellent customer service; through high productivity; through good-quality work

A4 by reducing errors and mistakes; this will also save costs, which may allow lower prices

***examiner's* note** A business can improve its competitiveness by offering similar benefits to others at a lower price or offering more benefits at the same price.

Competition

Q1 State two reasons why competition in a market may be limited.

Q2 If firms act against the public interest, this is called u................ c.................... Give an example of this type of behaviour.

Q3 State two possible benefits for the consumer of greater competition in a market.

Q4 If the number of firms in a market increases, does this change supply or demand?

A1 • if a patent exists
• if the market is expensive to enter
• government regulations

A2 unfair competition; examples are cartels and predatory pricing

A3 • lower prices
• better quality
• more choice

A4 with more firms in the market, supply increases

***examiner's* note** More competition in a market can act as an incentive to be more efficient; it may also lead to wasteful promotional activities.

The impact of more competition will vary between stakeholders, e.g. consumers may benefit from lower prices, but some firms may lose sales and profits.